Temple Prime

Account of Some of the Lines of the Princes of the Blood

of the House of France

Temple Prime

Account of Some of the Lines of the Princes of the Blood
of the House of France

ISBN/EAN: 9783337168834

Printed in Europe, USA, Canada, Australia, Japan

Cover: Foto ©ninafisch / pixelio.de

More available books at **www.hansebooks.com**

ACCOUNT

OF

SOME OF THE LINES OF THE

PRINCES OF THE BLOOD

OF THE

HOUSE OF FRANCE

BY

TEMPLE PRIME

NEW-YORK
1890

PRELIMINARY REMARKS.

The feudal nobility of France consisted of six classes: dukes, marquesses, counts, viscounts, barons, and chatelains.

Under the first races of sovereigns the offices of duke, marquess, and count were held by those to whom the King delegated authority in places at a distance from the court; dukes were charged with the government of provinces and had jurisdiction over a certain number of marquesses and counts; marquesses had charge of the frontiers, and counts of towns.

An edict of Charles IX. of 1566, provided that in all new creations of duchies, marquisates, and counties they should on failure of male issue revert to the crown; this provision of the edict, however, soon became a dead letter, as already in 1571 it was customary to insert in the letters a waiver of the forfeiture.

DUKES AND DUCHIES.

Dukes date back to the last period of the Roman empire, and derive their name from the word "Dux," leader of armies; this dignity, which originally was purely military, occupied in the imperial hierarchy the most exalted rank; later it was conferred upon the representatives of the Cæsars and upon governors of provinces.

The Franks retained the title, and their conquests were divided into duchies and counties; but though dukes and counts exercised the most extensive military and civil authority, they were simply officers at will.

Already, however, in the VIIIth century, some dukes, notably those of Aquitaine and Gascony, had made themselves independent.

Charles Martel undertook a crusade against the refractory dukes, but he succeeded only in so far that, while they recognized his suzerainty, the office remained hereditary.

Charlemagne compelled the dukes to submit to his authority; but after his death they soon regained their former power.

The accession to the throne of Hugues Capet, Duke of France, through the assistance of the dukes, naturally led to the recognition of their asserted rights.

France contained at that time the following duchies:
Aquitaine or Guienne (Rainulf, first duke, 845; since 850
a county);
Toulouse (Chosson, first duke, 778);
Burgundy (Henry, first duke, 970);
Brittany (Geoffrey, first duke, 992);
Normandy (Rollo, first duke, 876).

During some centuries no new duchies were added to the
list, and the first created were in favor of members of the
royal house; the first case was that of the duchy of Bour-
bon, erected in 1327 in favor of Louis, Count of Clermont.
Down to the year 1519 the following duchies were re-
created:
Burgundy, 1360;
Normandy, 1468;
Guienne, 1469.
And the following new ones were created:
Orleans, 1344;
Bar, 1354;
Anjou, Berry, Auvergne, and Touraine, 1360;
Nemours, 1404;
Valois, 1406;
Alençon, 1414;
Valentinois, 1498;
Longueville, 1505;
Angoulême, Vendôme, Châtellerault, 1514.

All these renewals and new creations were in favor of
members and connections of the royal house, except those
of Bar and Valentinois, the former being for a prince of
Lorraine, and the latter for Cæsar Borgia.

In 1519 we have the first instance of a duchy being
created for a subject not a kinsman of the King, namely,
that of Roannais, which was created in favor of Arthur
Gouffier.

Formerly, when a duchy was created, it contained four
counties, and in accordance with the edicts of Charles IX
and Henry III, it was necessary that it should yield a reve-
nue of 8,000 écus; but already in the XVIth century all that

was required when a duchy was created was that the lordship should be one of some importance, and at times the fiction was resorted to of uniting under one head lordships situated in different provinces. As a duchy could not be placed under the suzerainty of another duchy, this difficulty was avoided when it was within the territory of an existing one by placing it under the suzerainty of the " Great Tower of the Louvre."

There were two kinds of duchies, the duché-pairie and the duché héréditaire.

I. The Duché-Pairie.[1]

The duché-pairie, as its name indicates, carried with it a peerage. In some cases the peerage might lapse although the duchy itself did not, as the case might be, according to the provisions of the erection.

II. The Duché Héréditaire.

Duchés héréditaires were of three kinds:

(a) The duché ordinaire, in which the succession was confined to heirs male;

(b) The duché mâle et femel, which in failure of heirs male descended in the female line;

(c) The duché femel, created for a female and descending as the case might be.

A duchy was created by letters-patent, which had to be submitted to the Parliament of Paris for registration within a year from the date of their issue, and when registered, to the Cour des Comptes. In case Parliament refused the registration of the letters-patent, they lapsed on the death of the grantee, unless revived by what were known as "Lettres de Surannation."

Under the last kings there existed also another kind of duke, but not of duchy, namely, the " duc à brevèt," simply a dignity, created for life.

---

[1] For list of duchés-pairie, see Pairies, page 25.

LIST OF DUCHÉS HÉRÉDITAIRES.

Aiguillon (Guienne).
Duplessis 1704–1800.
Albrêt (Gascony).
Henry II, king of Navarre 1555.
Angoulême.
Valois-Auvergne 1620–1653.
Auvergne.
Bourbon 1400–1527.
Ayen (   ).
Noailles 1737.
Bar.
Lorraine 1354–1735.
Beaufort (Champaign).
Montmorency-Luxemburg 1688–1689.[1]
Beaumont (Isle-of-France).
Montmorency-Luxemburg 1765–1878.
Beaumont-au-Maine (Maine).
Alençon and Bourbon-Vendôme 1543–1589.
Beaupréau (Anjou).
Bourbon-la-Roche-sur-Yon 1562–1578.
Bournonville (Boulonnais).
Bournonville 1600.
Broglie (Normandy).
Broglie 1742.
Carignan (Luxemburg).
Savoy-Carignan 1661–1734.
Chartres.
Rénée of France, duchess of Ferrara 1528–1575.
Anne of Este, duchess of Guise and Nemours 1575–1607.
Savoy-Nemours 1607–1623.
Chateauroux (Berry).
Claire Clémence of Maillé, princess of Condé 1639–1694.
Bourbon-Condé 1694.

---

[1] Name changed to Montmorency, see Montmorency, page 11.

Châtellerault (Poitou).
Bourbon 1515–1527.
Louisa of Savoy 1527–1531.
James Hamilton 2d earl of Arran 1548–1563.[1]
Diana, duchess of Angoulême 1563–1582.
Bourbon-Montpensier 1583–1627.
Anne Mary Louisa of Orleans 1627–1693.
Orleans 1693–1694.
Chatillon-sur-Loing (Orléannais).
Montmorency-Luxemburg 1696–1795.
Chevreuse (Isle-of-France).
Brosse 1545–1547.
Lorraine-Guise 1555–1612.
Albert 1657–1667.
Coigny (Normandy).
Coigny 1747–1787.[2]
Croy (Picardy).
Croy 1598–1612.
Damville (Normandy).
La Rochefoucault 1732.
Duras (Guienne).
Durfort 1689–1858.
Estouteville (Normandy).
Estouteville and Bourbon-Vendôme 1534–1546.
Orleans-Longueville.
Princes of Monaco.
Estampes (Beauce).
Anne of Pisseleu 1536–1565
John Casimir, count palatine of the Rhine 1576–1577.
Catherine of Lorraine-Guise, duchess of Montpensier
1580–1582.
Margaret of France, queen of Navarre 1582–1598.
Gabrielle of Estrèes 1598–1599.
Vendôme 1599–1712.

---

[1] The title of duke of Châtellerault is claimed and borne by both
the dukes of Abercorn and Hamilton.
[2] Erected into a peerage, see page 29.
2

Gisors (Normandy).
Fouquet 1742–1748.
Harcourt (Normandy).
Harcourt 1700–1710.[1]
Hostun (Dauphiny).
Hostun 1712–1715.[2]
Humières (Artois).
Crévant 1690–1708.
Laforce (Guienne).
Nompar de Caumont 1787–1838.
Larocheguyon (Vexin).
La Rochefoucault 1679–1713.
Lauzun (Guienne).
Nompar de Caumont 1692–1723.
Laval (Maine).
Montmorency-Luxemburg 1758–1851.
Lévis (Bourbonnais).
Lévis 1784.
Longueville (Normandy).
Orleans-Longueville 1505–1694.
Lorges[3] (Brittany).
Durfort 1706–1770.
Durfort-Civrac 1773.
Loudun (Poitou).
Frances of Rohan 1580.
Maillé (Brittany).
Maillé 1784.
Mercoeur (Auvergne).
Mary Anne of Bourbon, duchess dowager of Vendôme
1712–1718.
Anne of Bavaria, princess dowager of Condé 1718–
1723.
Bourbon-Conty 1723–1770.
Montargis (Orléannais).
Rénée of France, duchess of Ferrara 1528–1575.

---

[1] Erected into a peerage, see page 31.
[2] Erected into a peerage, see page 31.
[3] See Quintin, page 11.

Anne of Este, duchess of Guise and Nemours 1575–1607.

Lorraine-Guise 1607–1612.

Monfort (Isle of France).

Albert 1692.

Montmorency [1] (Champaign).

Montmorency-Luxemburg 1689.

Nemours (Gastinois).

Graville 1477–1491.

Medici 1515–1528.

Savoy-Nemours 1528–1659.

Pont-de-Vaux (Bresse).

Gorrevod 1627–1681.

Quintin [2] (Brittany).

Durfort 1691–1706.

Roannais (Forez).

Gouffier 1566–1612.[3]

Aubusson 1667.[4]

Royan (Saint-Onge).

La Trémoille 1707–1733.

Thouars (Poitou).

La Trémoille 1563–1595.[5]

Uzès (Languedoc).

Crussol 1565–1573.[6]

Valentinois (Dauphiny).

Cæsar Borgia 1498–1507.

Diana of Poitiers 1548–1571.

Ventadour (Limousin).

Lévis 1578–1594.[7]

Villemor (Champaign).

Séguier 1650–1672.

---

[1] See Beaufort, page 8.
[2] Name changed to Lorges. see Lorges, page 10.
[3] Erected into a peerage, see page 34.
[4] Erected into a peerage, see page 34.
[5] Erected into a peerage, see page 35.
[6] Erected into a peerage, see page 35.
[7] Erected into a peerage, see page 36.

Villequier (Normandy).
Aumont 1759.
Villars (Isle-of-France).
Villars 1705–1709.[1]
Villars-Brancas (Provence).
Brancas 1627–1652.[2]

PRINCES AND PRINCIPALITIES.

The title of prince was originally confined to members of the royal house, and of sovereign houses domiciled in France, such as Lorraine, Savoy, Cleves, Gonzaga, etc.; in time, however, the title was assumed by members of the higher nobility.

The subject may be treated under two heads: "Principalities constituted by Ancient Usage or Creation," and "Fiefs which have furnished the Title of Prince to Members of the Royal and other Houses."

List of Principalities constituted by Ancient Usage or Creation.

Antibes (Provence), ancient sirerie with the title of principality; ceded to France in 1608.

Arches, or Charleville (Champaign), formerly a possession of the counts of Réthel, from whom it passed to the house of Gonzaga.

Argentan (Berry), principality since the Xth century.

Béarn, sovereign principality; united to France on the accession of Henry IV.

---

[1] Erected into a peerage, see page 36.
[2] Erected into a peerage, see page 36.

Bidache (Béarn), a possession of the house of Aure; furnishes the title to the head of the same, the duke of Gramont.

Charleville, see Arches.

Chateau-Porcien (Champaign), erected into a principality in 1561 in favor of the house of Croy; the house of Gonzaga held it from 1608 to 1688, when it passed to that of la Porte.

Chateau-Renaud (Champaign), formerly a possession of the counts of Réthèl; purchased by the crown in 1629.

Déols (Berry), ancient principality.

Dombes, sovereign principality; purchased by the crown in 1762.

Donzère (Dauphiny), formerly owned by the bishops of Verviers.

Enrichemont, see Henrichemont.

Espinoy (Artois), erected into a principality by the emperor Charles V in 1545 in favor of the house of Melun; owned since 1714 by the house of Rohan-Soubise.

Graçay (Berry), principality since the IXth century.

Guémené (Brittany), erected into a principality in 1570 in favor of the house of Rohan.

Henrichemont, or Enrichemont (Berry); in 1598 the fiefs of Henrichemont and Boisbelle were united and erected into a principality in favor of the house of Béthune.

Joinville (Champaign), sirerie erected into a principality in 1551 in favor of the house of Lorraine-Guise.

Issoudun (Berry), principality since the Xth century.

Ivetot (Normandy), very ancient principality.

Linières (Berry), principality since the XIth century.

Martigues (Provence), erected into a principality by Henry IV in favor of Mary of Luxemburg, duchess of Mercoeur; passed by descent to the house of Vendôme; sold 1714 to the house of Villars.

Mercoeur (Auvergne), erected into a principality in 1569 in favor of Nicholas of Lorraine; erected into a duché-pairie in his favor in 1576.

Orange, sovereign principality; ceded to France in 1713

by the Treaty of Utrecht; furnishes the title to the branch of the house of Nassau reigning in the Netherlands.

Phalsburg (Lorraine), erected by the emperor Ferdinand III into a principality in favor of Henrietta of Lorraine, sister of Charles IV, duke of Lorraine.

Sedan, sovereign principality; ceded to France in 1642.

Tingry (Picardy), erected into a principality in 1587 in favor of the duke of Piney; has furnished the title of prince to members of the houses of Montmorency-Luxemburg and Albert.

List of Fiefs which have furnished the Title of Prince to Members of the Royal and other Houses.

Amblise (Belgium) furnished the title to members of the house of Anglure.

Anet (Chartrain) styled principality in the XVIth century, when it passed to the house of Lorraine-Aumale; no one has borne the title as a principal one.

Bouillon (Belgium) furnished the title to members of the house of la Tour d'Auvergne.

Bournonville (Bolounnais) furnished the title to members of the house of Henin.

Carency (Artois) styled principality from having at one time been in the possession and furnished the title to members of the house of Bourbon-Carency.

Carignan (Luxemburg) furnished the title to the house of Savoy-Carignan.

Chabannais (Angoumois) furnished the title to members of the first house of Vendôme.

Chalais (Périgord) furnished the title to members of the house of Talleyrand.

Chatelaillon (Poitou) furnished the title to Louis I of Orleans, duke of Longueville.

Commercy (Lorraine) furnished the title to a member of the house of Lorraine-Lillebonne.

Condé (Brie) furnished the title to the house of Bourbon-Condé; from 1845 to 1866 to Louis Philip of Orleans son of the duke of Aumale.

Conty (Picardy) furnished the title to the house of Bourbon-Conty.

Elbeuf (Normandy) furnished the title to members of the house of Lorraine-Elbeuf.

Grimberg (Belgium) furnished the title to members of the house of Albert.

Guise (County of Guise-sur-Moselle, Lorraine) furnished the title to members of the house of Lorraine-Harcourt.

Harcourt (Normandy) furnished the title to members of the house of Lorraine-Harcourt.

Isle-sur-Montréal (Languedoc) furnished the title to members of the house of Maillé.

Lamballe (Brittany) furnished the title from 1747 to 1768 to Louis-Alexander of Bourbon-Toulouse son of the duke of Penthièvre.

Lambesc (Provence) furnished the title to members of the house of Lorraine-Armagnac.

La-Roche-sur-Yon, see Roche-sur-Yon.

Léon (Brittany) furnishes the title to members of the house of Rohan-Chabot.

Lixheim, see Lixin.

Lixin or Lixheim (Lorraine) furnished the title to a member of the house of Lorraine-Elbeuf.

Marcillac (Angoumois) furnished the title to members of the house of la Rochefoucault.

Maubuisson (Isle-of-France) furnished the title to members of the houses of Lévis and Rohan.

Montauban (Brittany) furnishes the title to members of the house of Rohan.

Montbazon (Touraine) furnishes the title to members of the house of Rohan.

Montlaur (Dauphiny) furnished the title to members of the houses of Créqui and Lorraine-Harcourt.

Montmorency[1] (Champaign) furnished the title to members of a junior line of the house of Montmorency.

Mortagne (Saint-Onge) furnished the title to members of the house of Lorraine-Harcourt.

Poix (Picardy) furnished the title to members of the house of Créqui; and now to members of a junior branch of the house of Noailles.

Pons (Saint-Onge) furnished the title to members of the house of Albert.

Raucourt (Luxemburg) furnished the title to members of the house of la Tour d'Auvergne.

Rochefort (Brittany) furnishes the title to members of the house of Rohan.

Roche-sur-Yon, (la), (Poitou) furnished the title to members of the houses of Bourbon-la-Roche-sur-Yon and Bourbon-Conty.

Rubenpré (Belgium) furnished the title to members of the house of Maillé.

Soubise (Brittany) furnishes the title to members of the house of Rohan.

Soyons (Vivarais) furnished the title to members of the house of Crussol and to the bishops of Valence.

Talmond (Saint-Onge) furnishes the title to members of the house of la Trémoille.

Tancarville (Normandy) furnished the title to members of the house of Montmorency-Luxemburg.

Tarente (Italy) furnishes the title to members of the house of la Trémoille.

Tonnay-Charente (Saint-Onge) furnishes the title to members of the house of Rochechouart.

Turenne (Auvergne) furnished the title to members of the house of la Tour d'Auvergne.

Vaudemont (Lorraine) furnished the title to members of the house of Lorraine.

Vergaigne (Spain) furnished the title in 1709 to a member of the house of Mazarin.

---

[1] Originally Beaufort, name changed in 1689.

PRINCES OF THE ROYAL HOUSE.

The subject may be treated under two heads: "Princes belonging to the Immediate Family of the Sovereign" and "Princes of the Blood."

Princes belonging to the Immediate Family of the Sovereign.

This class consisted of the King's sons, his brothers, and the sons of the Dauphin; they alone were styled "Royal Highness" and bore the patronymic "France"; they were respectively "children" and "grandchildren of France."

From the time of Philip VI, the King's second son received, when not already occupied, the title of duke of Orleans, the third son that of duke of Anjou, and the fourth that of duke of Berry.

Princes of the Blood.

Princes of the blood were the descendants of the younger sons and of the brothers of the King; they bore as patronymic the name of the title of their immediate ancestor. The member of this entire class, the nearest in the line of succession to the crown, was styled "first prince of the blood."

The following are instances of this class:

Robert, count of Dreux, son of Louis VI, founded the line of that name, extinct in 1514.

Robert, count of Artois, son of Louis VIII, founded the line of that name, extinct in 1472.

Charles, count of Anjou, son of Louis VIII, founded a line of that name, extinct in 1435.

Robert, count of Clermont, son of Louis IX, was founder of a line which bore originally the name of Cler-

3

mont, but that county having been returned to the crown, the counts took that of Bourbon, of which fief they were dukes. This line came to the throne in 1589.

Louis, count of Évreux, son of Philip III, founded the line of that name, extinct in 1441.

Charles, count of Valois, son of Philip III, founded the lines of Valois and Alençon.

Louis, duke of Anjou, son of John II, founded a line of that name, extinct in 1481.

John, duke of Berry, son of John II, founded the line of that name, extinct in 1416.

Philip, duke of Burgundy, son of John II, founded the second line of Burgundy, extinct in 1491.

Louis, duke of Orleans, son of Charles V, founded the first line of Orleans, which came to the throne in 1498.

Philip, duke of Orleans, son of Louis XIII, founded the present house of Orleans.

By the edict of 1576, princes of the King's family and princes of the blood who were peers took precedence of all other peers; by the edict of 1711, these princes, whether peers or not, took precedence of all peers.

MARQUISATES.

Marquisates by virtue of the edicts of Charles IX and Henry III were required to consist of three baronies and six chatellenies, and were held immediately of the crown. But one marquisate, that of Coucy, had a peerage connected with it.

COUNTIES AND COUNTS.

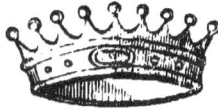

Counties under the edicts of Charles IX and Henry III contained two baronies and three chatellenies, or one barony and six chatellenies.

There were formerly two kinds of counts, the count who exercised jurisdiction under a duke, and the count palatine of France.

Counts palatine of France, called also counts of the palace, derived their name from the fact that originally they administered justice in the palace of the King.

The count of Champaign was the first count to adopt the designation of " Count palatine of France," to show that he received his investiture from the King of France and not from the Emperor.

Counts palatine date back to the early days of the Frankish monarchy and still existed under the third race.

The principal French counties palatine were those of Champaign, Guienne, Flanders, and Toulouse.

VISCOUNTIES AND VISCOUNTS.

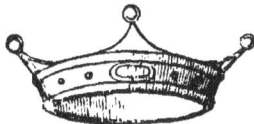

No law regulated the number of fiefs necessary to constitute a viscounty. There is no instance of a viscounty with a peerage connected with it.

There were three kinds of viscounts: those who exercised their functions under a count, those who exercised their functions under a count palatine, and those who held their viscounties immediately of the King, such as the viscounts of Turenne and Melun.

BARONIES.

Baronies under the edicts of Charles IX and Henry III had to contain no less than three chatellenies.

There were two kinds of baronies, the ordinary one held of a higher fief, and the barony of France, or sirerie, held immediately of the King.

There were but few sireries, the most prominent were those of Coucy, Bourbon, Beaujeu, Joinville, and Sully.

In time the name of sireric disappeared, from the fact that the sireries fell to the crown or that their holders were raised in rank.

CHATELLENIES.

A chatellenie under the edicts of Charles IX and Henry III, was a fief having "haute," "moyenne," and "basse justice."

VIDAMERIES AND VIDAMES.

There was still another class of nobility, which had, however, a very limited membership, that of the vidames. A

vidame was formerly the officer charged with the adminis-
tration of justice in a bishopric and of caring for many of
the temporal matters of the see, more especially of military
matters.

In time vidameries became fiefs and were hereditary.

A vidamerie took its name from the bishopric with which
it was connected, and was held of the same, with the excep-
tion of the vidamerie of Normandy, which was held of the
crown.

The vidamerie of Gerberoy was annexed to the bishopric
of Beauvais, the bishop being vidame of Gerberoy.

Later all practical connection between vidameries and
bishoprics ceased.

THE APPANAGE.

An appanage was the provision made by the crown for
a prince of the royal house in order to enable him to main-
tain his dignity.

The first six Kings of the third race in order to guarantee
the succession to the entire realm to their elder sons, took
the precaution of having them "sacré" while still on the
throne and shared with them from that time forward the
exercise of the royal power. In course of time the prin-
ciple of the succession of the eldest son became a fixed
usage and law; but as under this arrangement no provision
was made for the junior members of the royal house, the
system of the appanage was introduced.

As Rageau defines it: "In the house of France there is
no partage, but there is appanage, and this only since the
accession of the third line of Kings; prior to that time there
was partage of the empire."

Under some of the early Kings of the third race, the
crown domain was of such limited extent that the King
could give the princes but very meagre appanages, and in
some cases none at all. The King, therefore, endeavored to

marry the princes to the heiresses of great houses; *e. g.*, Hugo, son of Henry I, married the heiress of Vermandois; Peter, son of Louis VI, the heiress of Courtenai; Philip, son of Philip II, the heiress of Boulogne, and, finally, Robert, son of Louis IX, the heiress of Bourbon.

In the early times the reversion of the appanage was subject to no fixed law, but depended upon the good will of the grantor. Originally the appanage was granted in fee simple, later a clause of reversion was added, and shortly afterwards the succession to the appanage was restricted to heirs male.

There are three epochs in the history of appanages: first from Hugues Capet, 987, to Philip II, 1180; second from Louis VIII, 1223, to Philip IV, 1285, and third from Philip IV to the Revolution.

During the first period there appear to have been no stipulations regarding reversion; during the second period, appanages increasing in number, some rules were adopted, introducing and regulating reversion. In the grants of appanages under Louis IX it was laid down, that should the appanagee leave no heir of his body (sine herede corporis sui) the appanage was to revert to the crown; in default of heirs male, females could succeed.

After the reversion to the crown, under Louis XI of Burgundy and Provence, and the acquisition of Brittany in 1532, there were no longer any great vassals of the crown; many of the original appanages had lapsed, and the privileges and jurisdictions possessed by the nobles, although still in many cases very great, were thereafter held and exercised in strict subordination to the royal authority.

In 1566 Charles IX issued an edict settling the status of appanages; this edict was in the nature of a statute declaratory, giving the force of written law to usages existing from the time of Charles V. This is the first written enactment limiting rights of appanages and subjecting them to definite rules.

The edict of 1566 recognized but two kinds of alienation of the royal domain, that of "appanage" and that of "engagement," and stipulated for the reversion of the appanage on the extinction of the male line.

When the appanagee died he was succeeded by the heir male, the succession being based upon the same rules that governed that to the crown. In case the appanagee came to the throne, his appanage reverted to the crown and did not pass to the next senior member of the new King's house, when such existed; *e. g.*, when Louis of Orleans duke of Orleans became King under the name of Louis XII, his appanage did not pass to the next senior member of the house of Orleans, the count of Angoulême, but returned to the domain.

In order the better to understand the nature of an appanage, it is desirable to consider the other form of alienation of the crown domain authorized by the edict of Charles IX, namely the " engagement."

"Engagement" was a sale by the crown of a portion of the royal domain, subject to a perpetual right of redemption, carrying with it the " droits utiles "but not the " droits honorifiques."

The appanagee became seized of all the honorary titles attached to the fiefs forming his appanage; he could style himself duke, count, etc., as the case might be, according to the rank of his fiefs; but the " engagiste " was not authorized to do so, he could only style himself lord by " engagement " of such and such a fief.

The appanagee was entitled to all the feudal rights attached to his lordships, as well " utiles " as " honorifiques"; the latter were denied to the " engagiste," remaining vested in the crown.

In the lands of the appanagee justice was administered in his name, whereas in those of the " engagiste," it ran in the name of the King.

The " engagiste " had one advantage over the appanagee, his interest could be alienated; the appanagee was not allowed to alienate any portion of the appanage; should he however grant a part of the same to junior members of his house, which he was allowed to do, it could not leave their hands, and on their death without issue, it reverted to him, and should he ascend the throne, the whole appanage had to be forthcoming, to return to the royal domain.

THE PEERAGE.

The peerage was of two kinds, ecclesiastical and lay, and embraced five orders of fiefs: duchies, marquisates, counties, baronies, and chatellenies.

Originally there were but thirteen peerages, six ecclesiastical, to wit:

> the archbishopric duchy of Rheims,
> the bishopric duchy of Laon,
> the bishopric duchy of Langres,
> the bishopric county of Beauvais,
> the bishopric county of Chalons,
> the bishopric county of Noyon;

and seven lay ones, to wit:

> the duchy of France,
> the duchy of Burgundy,
> the duchy of Guienne,
> the duchy of Normandy,
> the county of Champaign,
> the county of Toulouse,
> the county of Flanders.

When Hugues Capet duke of France ascended the throne in 987 the duchy of France was returned to the crown domain, and the number of lay peerages was reduced to six.

After the crown had absorbed the remaining six lay peerages, it created new ones, and later even revived some of the original ones. Originally these new creations were only in favor of members of the royal house; in course of time, however, they were extended to ordinary subjects.

The first prince created peer under the new order of things was John of Dreux, in whose favor the duchy of

Brittany was erected into a peerage in 1297; the first ordinary subject made a peer was Arthur Gouffier, who was created duke peer of Roannais in 1519.

The number of lay peerages went on increasing, and when Henry III came to the throne in 1574 there were eight, which at the time of his death in 1589 had grown to eighteen. Peerages became so numerous under succeeding reigns that at the breaking out of the Revolution the order had lost much of its prestige.

The original lay peers took an active part in the ceremony of the King's coronation; on the extinction of these peerages these functions were not exercised by new peers, but by deputy, in the name of the original peers.

A lay[1] peerage, under the new order of things, was erected by letters patent and the same formalities were pursued as in the erection of a duchy.

Lay peerages descended in the manner prescribed by the letters patent. As a rule, however, the descent was confined to the male line.

All peers had seats in the parliament of Paris.

LIST OF ECCLESIASTICAL PEERAGES.

Beauvais (bishopric county).
Chalons (bishopric county).
Langres (bishopric duchy).
Laon (bishopric duchy).
Noyon (bishopric county).
Rheims (archbishopric duchy).

LIST OF LAY PEERAGES.

Duchies.

Aiguillon (Guienne).
Lorraine-Guise 1600–1621.

---

[1] No new ecclesiastical peerage was ever created.

4

L'Age 1634–1635.
Vignerot 1638–1704.
Albrêt (Gascony).
Albrêt 1550–1556.
Bourbon-Vendôme 1556–1589.
la Tour d'Auvergne 1652.
Bourbon-Condé 1662.
Alençon[1] (Normandy).
Alençon 1415–1524.
Francis of France, duke of Alençon 1566–1584.
Charles of France, duke of Berry 1710–1714.
Louis XVIII 1774–1793.
Angoulême[2] (Angoumois).
Louisa of Savoy, 1515–1531.
Charles of France, duke of Orleans 1540–1545.
Charles of France, duke of Berry 1710–1714.
Charles X 1773–1824.
Anjou.[3]
Anjou 1360–1480.
Henry III 1566–1574.
Francis of France, duke of Alençon 1576–1584.
Louis XVIII 1771–1793.
Antin (Guienne).
Pardaillan 1711–1757.
Arpajon (Languedoc and Guienne).
Arpajon 1650–1679.
Aubigny (Berry).
Quérouaille and Lenox 1684.

---

[1] The title of duke of Alençon was borne in 1713 by Charles of Berry, son of Charles of France, duke of Berry; it is now borne by Ferdinand of Orleans, second son of the duke of Nemours.

[2] The title of duke of Angoulême was borne from 1775 to 1824 by the Dauphin, son of Charles X.

[3] The title of duke of Anjou was borne by Gaston of France, duke of Orleans 1608–1626; Philip of France, duke of Orleans 1640–1661; Philip, son of Louis XIV 1668–1671; Louis Francis son of Louis XIV 1672; Philip V King of Spain 1683–1700; Louis XV 1710–1712; a son of Louis XV 1730–1733.

Aumale (Normandy).
    Lorraine-Guise 1547-1595.
    Savoy-Nemours 1631-1659.
    Bourbon-Maine 1695-1775.
    Bourbon-Toulouse 1775-1793.
    Orleans 1793.
Aumont (Champaign).
    Aumont 1665.
Auvergne.
    John of France, duke of Berry 1360-1400.
    Charles X 1773-1824.
Beaufort (Champaign).
    Estrées and Vendôme 1597-1712.
Berry.[1]
    John of France, duke of Berry 1340-1416.
    John of France 1416-1417.
    Charles VII 1417-1422.
    Charles of France, duke of Berry 1461-1472.
    Margaret, queen of Navarre 1517-1549.
    Francis of France, duke of Alençon 1576-1584.
    Charles X 1776-1824.
Bellegarde (Burgundy).
    Saint-Lary 1620-1646.
Béthune (Flanders).
    Béthune 1652-1678.
Biron (Périgordais).
    Gontaut 1598-1602.
    Gontaut 1723-1793.
Boufflers (Beauvoisis).
    Boufflers 1708-1747.
Bourbon.
    Bourbon 1327-1527.
    Charles of France, duke of Orleans 1543-1545.
    Henry III 1566-1574.

---

[1] The title of duke of Berry was borne from 1668 to 1714 by Charles of France, grandson of Louis XIV; from 1754 to 1765 by Louis XVI, and from 1778 to 1820 by Charles Ferdinand of Artois, second son of Charles X.

Bourbon-Condé 1662–1830.
Henry of Orleans, duke of Aumale 1830.

Bournonville (Boulonnais).
Bournonville 1652–1693.

Brienne (Champaign).
Luxemburg 1587–1605.

Brissac (Anjou).
Cossé 1611.

Brittany.[1]
Dreux 1297–1532.

Burgundy.[2]
Burgundy 1001–1361.
Burgundy 1363–1477.

Candale (   ).
Nogaret 1611–1620.

Cardonne (Catalonia).
La Motte-Houdancourt 1652–1657.

Charost (Berry).
Béthune 1673–1800.

Chartres.
Gaston of France, duke of Orleans 1626–1660.
Orleans 1661–1830.

Chateauroux (Berry).
Bourbon-Condé 1616.
Charles X 1776–1824.

Chateauvillain (Champaign).
L'Hopital 1650–1679.
Bourbon-Toulouse 1703–1793.
Orleans 1793.

Chateauthierry (Champaign).
Francis of France, duke of Alençon 1566–1584.
la Tour d'Auvergne 1652.

---

[1] The title of duke of Brittany was borne from 1532 to 1536 by Francis, eldest son of Francis I; from 1539 to 1546 by Henry II; from 1704 to 1705 and from 1707 to 1712 by two older brothers of Louis XV.

[2] The title of duke of Burgundy was borne from 1682 to 1711 by the father of Louis XV, and from 1751 to 1761 by Louis Joseph Xavier of France, older brother of Louis XVI.

Châtellerault (Poitou).
Bourbon 1515-1527.
Charles of France, duke of Orleans 1540-1545.
Chatillon (Poitou).
Chatillon 1736-1762.
Chatillon-sur-Loing [1] (Orléannais).
Coligny 1646-1649.
Chaulnes (Picardy).
Albert 1621-1698.
Albert 1711.
Chevreuse (Isle-of-France).
Lorraine-Guise 1627-1657.
Albert 1667.
Choiseul (Burgundy and Champaign).
Choiseul 1665-1705.
Clermont-Tonnerre (Burgundy).
Clermont-Tonnerre 1571-1573.
Clermont-Tonnerre 1775.
Coigny (Normandy).
Franquetot 1787-1865.
Coislin (Brittany).
Cambout 1663-1732.
Coligny [2] (Orléannais).
Coligny 1643-1646.
Coulomniers (Brie).
Orleans-Longueville 1656-1663.
Créquy (Picardy).
Blanchefort 1653-1687.
Damville (Normandy).
Montmorency 1610-1632.
Bourbon-Toulouse 1694-1719.
Dunois (Orléannais).
Orleans-Longueville 1525-1536.
Duras (Guienne).
Durfort 1668-1704.

---

[1] See Coligny.
[2] Name changed to Chatillon-sur-Loing, see same.

Elbeuf (Normandy).
Lorraine-Guise 1581–1825.
Enghien [1] (Isle-of-France).
Bourbon-Condé 1567–1569.
Bourbon-Condé 1689–1830.
Henry of Orleans, duke of Aumale 1830.
Epernon (Chartrain).
Nogaret 1581–1661.
Estrèes (Soissonnais).
Estrèes 1663–1737.
Evreux (Normandy).
Francis of France, duke of Alençon 1569–1584.
Fitz-James (Beauvoisis).
Fitz-James 1710.
Fleury (Languedoc).
Rosset 1736–1815.
Fronsac (Guienne).
Orleans-Longueville 1609–1631.
Duplessis 1634–1643.
Maillé 1643–1646.
Duplessis 1646.
Frontenay (Saint-Onge).
Rohan 1626–1640.
Gesvres (   ).
Potier 1670–1794.
Gisors (Normandy).
Fouquet 1748–1761.
Gramont (Gascony).
Aure 1648.
Grancey (Champaign).
Hautemer 1611–1613.
Graville (Normandy).
Charles of Bourbon-Condé, Cardinal of Bourbon
1567–1594.
Guienne.
Guienne Xth Century 1204.
Plantagenet 1204–1259.

Louis of France, son of Charles VI, 1401–1415.
Charles of France, duke of Berry 1469–1472.

Guise (Picardy).
Lorraine-Guise 1528-1675.
Bourbon-Condé 1704–1830.
Henry of Orleans, duke of Aumale 1830.[1]

Halwyn (Picardy).
Halwyn 1588–1591.
Halwyn and Nogaret 1611–1620.
Halwyn and Schomberg 1620–1656.

Harcourt (Normandy).
Harcourt 1710.

Hostun (Dauphiny).
Hostun 1715; extinct.

Joyeuse (Gévaudan).
Joyeuse 1581–1656.
Lorraine-Guise 1656–1688.
Melun 1714–1724.

la Ferté (Orléannais).
Saint-Nectaire 1665–1705.

la Force (Guienne).
Caumont 1637–1755.

la Meilleraye (Poitou).
la Porte 1663–1738.

la Rochefoucault (Angoumois).
la Rochefoucault 1622.

la Rocheguyon (Vexin).
Duplessis 1663–1674.

la Valette (Angoumois).
Nogaret 1631–1661.

la Vallière (Anjou).
la Baume-le-Blanc and Mary Anne of Bourbon, princess of Conty 1667–1688.
la Baume-le-Blanc 1723–1780.

---

[1] The title of duke of Guise has been borne by the following sons of the duke of Aumale : Henry of Orleans 1847.
Francis of Orleans 1852.
Francis of Orleans 1854–1872.

la Vauguyon (Guienne).

    quélen 1758–1839.

Lavedan [1] (Gascony).

    Montault 1650–1654.

    Montault 1654–1660.

la Vieuxville (Champaign).

    la Vieuxville 1650–1689.

Lesdiguières (Dauphiny).

    Bonne and Créquy 1620–1711.

Lévis (Bourbonnais).

    Lévis 1723–1734.

Louvois ( ).

    Adelaide and Victoire of France 1776–1800.

le Lude (Anjou).

    Daillon 1675–1685.

Luynes (Touraine).

    Albert 1619.

Mayenne (Normandy).

    Lorraine-Guise 1573–1621.

Mazarin (Champaign).

    la Porte 1663–1799.

Mercœur (Auvergne).

    Lorraine-Mercœur 1576–1603.

    Vendôme 1603–1712.

    Charles X 1773–1824.

Montault [2] (Gascony).

    Montault 1660–1684.

Montausier (Angoumois).

    Sainte-Maure 1665–1690.

Montbazon (Touraine).

    Rohan 1588–1589.

    Rohan 1594.

Montmirail [3] (Vendée).

    la Trémoille 1657–1666.

---

[1] Name changed to Montault, see same.
[2] See Lavedan.
[3] See Noirmoutier.

Montmorency [1] (Isle-of-France).
Montmorency 1551–1632.
Bourbon-Condé 1633–1689.
Montpensier (Auvergne).
Bourbon-Montpensier 1538–1627.
Anne Mary Louisa of Orleans 1627–1693.
Orleans 1693.
Mortemart (Poitou).
Rochechouart 1650.
Nemours (Gastinois).
Charles III, King of Navarre 1404–1425.
Armagnac 1461–1469.
Armagnac 1491–1503.
Gaston of Foix 1507–1512.
Orleans 1672–1830.
Nevers (Nivernais).
Cleves 1539–1564.
Gonzaga 1566–1652.
Mazarin 1660–1661.
Mazarin 1676–1707.
Mazarin 1720–1798.
Noailles (Limousin).
Noailles 1663.
Noirmoutier [2] (Vendée).
La Trémoille 1650–1657.
Normandy. [3]
Normandy IXth Century — 1167.
Plantagenet 1167–1259.
John II 1332–1350.
Charles V 1355–1364.
Charles of France, duke of Berry 1465.
Orleans [4] (Orléannais).
Philip of France, duke of Orleans 1344–1375.

---

[1] Name changed to Enghien, see same.
[2] Name changed to Montmirail, see same.
[3] Louis XVII bore the title of duke of Normandy from 1785 to 1789.
[4] The title of duke of Orleans was borne by Henry II from 1519 to 1536; by Louis son of Henry II from 1548 to 1550; by Charles IX from 1550 to 1560, and by the second son of Henry IV from 1607 to 1611.

5

Orleans 1362-1498.
Charles of France, duke of Orleans 1540-1545.
Gaston of France, duke of Orleans 1626-1660.
Orleans 1661-1830.

Penthièvre [1] (Brittany).
Luxemburg 1569-1623.
Lorraine-Mercœur 1623-1669.
Vendôme 1669-1687.
Bourbon-Toulouse 1697-1793.
Orleans 1793.

Piney (Bassigny).
Luxemburg 1581-1615.
Albert 1630-1698.
Montmorency-Luxemburg 1698-1861.

Praslin (Isle-of-France).
Choiseul 1762.

Puylaurens (Languedoc).
L'Age 1634-1635.

Rambouillet (Isle-of-France).
Bourbon-Toulouse 1711-1783.

Randan (Auvergne).
La Rochefoucault and Foix 1663-1714.

Rèthelois (Champaign).
Gonzaga 1581-1652.

Retz (Brittany).
Gondi 1583-1659.
Gondi 1659-1676.

Richelieu (Poitou).
Duplessis 1631-1821.

Roannais (Forez).
Gouffier 1519.
Gouffier 1612.
Aubusson 1667-1725.

Rohan (Brittany).
Rohan 1603-1638.
Rohan-Chabot 1648-1787.

---

[1] The title of duke of Penthièvre was borne by Charles of Orleans, son of Louis Philip, from 1820 to 1828; it is now borne by Peter of Orleans, son of the prince of Joinville.

Rohan-Rohan (Saint-Onge).
Rohan 1714.
Roquelaure (Languedoc).
Roquelaure 1652–1683.
Roquelaure 1683–1748.
Rosnay (Champaign).
L'Hôpital 1651–1660.
Saint-Aignan (Berry).
Beauvilliers 1663–1828.
Saint-Cloud (Isle-of-France).
The archbishops of Paris 1674.
Saint-Fargeau (Orléannais).
Bourbon-Montpensier 1575–1627.
Anne Mary Louisa of Orleans 1627–1693.
Saint-Simon (Vermandois).
Rouvroy 1635–1755.
Stainville (   ).
Choiseul 1759–1785.
Sully (Sologne).
Béthune 1606–1807.
Thouars (Poitou).
la Trémoille 1595.
Touraine.
Philip of France, duke of Burgundy 1360–1363.
Louis of France, duke of Anjou 1363.
Louis of France, duke of Orleans 1386–1392.
John, son of Charles VI, 1401–1416.
Charles VII 1416–1422.
Archibald, 4th earl of Douglass 1423–1424.
Louis III of Anjou, King of Sicily 1424–1434.
Francis of France, duke of Alençon 1576–1584.
Tresmes (Poitou).
Potier 1648–1794.
Uzès (Languedoc).
Crussol 1573.
Valentinois (Dauphiny).
Monaco 1643–1730.
Valois (Isle-of-France).
Orleans 1406–1498.

Francis I 1498–1515.
Gaston of France, duke of Orleans 1630–1660.
Orleans 1661–1830.
Vendôme (Orléannais).
Bourbon-Vendôme 1514–1589.
Vendôme 1598–1712.
Ventadour (Limousin).
Lévis 1594–1717.
Verneuil (Isle-of-France).
Henry of Bourbon-Verneuil 1663–1682.
Villars (Isle-of-France).
Villars 1709–1770.
Villars-Brancas (Provence).
Brancas 1652–1822.
Villeroy (Gastinois).
Neufville 1651–1794.

MARQUISATE.

Coucy (Isle-of-France).
Orleans 1672–1830.

COUNTIES.

Angoulême (Angoumois).
Philip, King of Navarre 1325.
Orleans 1394–1515.
Anjou.
Anjou 1246–1328.
John II 1332–1350.

Artois.

Artois 1297; fell by descent to the house of Austria; ceded to France 1659.

Auxerre (Burgundy).

Burgundy 1435–1477.

Beaumont-le-Roger (Normandy).

Artois 1329–1332.

Philip of France, duke of Orleans 1332–1354.

Évreux 1355–1404.

Blois (Orléannais).

Gaston of France, duke of Orleans 1626–1660.

Champaign.

Champaign XIth Century — 1304.

Clermont (Beauvoisis).

Bourbon 1331–1527.

Charles of France, duke of Orleans 1540–1545.

Estampes (Beauce).

Évreux 1327–1400.

Foix 1478–1512.

Eu (Normandy).

Artois 1458–1472.

Burgundy 1472–1491.

Cleves 1491–1633.

Lorraine-Guise 1633–1660.

Anne Mary Louisa of Orleans 1660–1693.

Bourbon-Maine 1693–1775.

Bourbon-Toulouse 1775-1793.

Orleans 1793.

Évreux (Normandy).

Évreux 1313–1404.

John Stuart 1426–1429.

Flanders.

Flanders IXth Century — 1118.

Denmark 1118–1127.

Normandy 1127–1128.

Alsace 1128–1194.

Hainault 1194–1279.

Dampierre 1279–1404.

Burgundy 1404–1477.
Austria 1477.
Foix (Languedoc).
Gaston, count of Foix 1458–1483.
Forez.
Henry III 1566–1574.
Gisors (Normandy).
Francis of France, duke of Alençon 1566–1584.
Macon (Burgundy).
John of France, duke of Berry 1359–1360.
Burgundy 1435–1477.
Maine.
John II 1332–1350.
Anjou 1360–1481.
Louis XVIII 1771–1793.
Mante (Isle-of-France).
Charles, King of Navarre 1354–1365.
Francis of France, duke of Alençon 1566–1584.
Marche (la).
Charles IV 1316–1321.
Bourbon 1327–1435.
Armagnac 1435–1477.
Bourbon 1477–1527.
Charles of France, duke of Orleans 1540–1545.
Henry III 1566–1574.
Meulant (Isle-of-France).
Francis of France, duke of Alençon 1566–1584.
Mortain (Normandy).
Évreux 1325.
Évreux 1408–1012.
Louis, son of Charles VI, 1414–1415.
Charles of France, duke of Berry 1465–1472.
Nevers.
Louis III, count of Flanders 1347.
Burgundy-Nevers 1459–1491.
Cleves 1505–1539.
Perche (la).
Francis of France, duke of Alençon 1566–1584.

Périgord (Guienne).
>Louis of France, duke of Orleans 1400–1438.

Poitou.
>Philip V 1315–1316.
>John of France, duke of Berry 1357–1360.
>John of France, duke of Berry 1369–1416.
>Charles VII 1417–1422.

Ponthieu (Picardy).
>Charles of France, duke of Berry 1710–1714.

Rèthel (Champaign).
>Louis III, count of Flanders 1347.
>Anthony of Burgundy 1405.

Soissons.
>Orleans 1404–1498.
>Claude of France, Queen of France 1505–1515.

Toulouse.
>Toulouse VIIIth Century — 1271.

Valois (Isle-of-France).
>Philip of France, duke of Orleans 1344–1375.
>Orleans 1386–1406.

Villefranche (Rouergue).
>Frederick of Arragon 1480.

BARONIES.

Coucy (Isle-of-France).
>Orleans 1404–1489.
>Claude of France, Queen of France 1505–1515.

Donzy (Luxemburg).
>Louis III, count of Flanders 1347.

Montpellier (Languedoc).
>Évreux 1371–1382.

CHATELLENIES.

Mortagne (Flanders).
John, son of Charles VII 1407–1416.
Vernon (Normandy).
Francis of France, duke of Alençon 1566–1584.

BIBLIOGRAPHY.

De la commodité de l'apanage et partage de M. M. les enfans de France; Vaillant 1585. 8°.

Histoire des dignitez honoraires de France; Lazarre 1635. 8°.

La France seigneuriale; Duval 1650. 12°.

Recueil des droits du roi; Dupuy 1655; fol.

Bibliothèque du droit français; Bouchel 1667; fol.

Des partages et apanages des enfans de France; Husson 1677; fol.

Mémoires de Trévoux 1708.

Recueil d'édits, déclarations et arrets concernant la noblesse, depuis 1566 jusqu'a 1712. 2 vols., 4°.

Essai sur la noblesse de France; de Boulainvilliers 1732. 12°.

Histoire de la pairie et du parlement de Paris; de Boulainvilliers 1733. 2 vols., 12°.

Traité de la noblesse; de la Roque 1734. 4°.

Histoire de la pairie de France; de B. (du Boullay) 1740. sm. 8°.

Dissertation sur l'origine etc. des pairs de France; Simonel 1753. 12°.

Chronologie des duchés-pairies et des comtés-pairies; (Chazaud de Nantigny) 1753. 4°.

Mémoires sur les matières domaniales; Lefèvre de la Planche 1764. 3 vols., 4°.

G   41

Dictionnaire généalogique; M. D. L. C. D. B. (Aubert de la Chesnayes des Bois) 1770. 4°.

Les quatre ages de la pairie de France; Zemgans (Goezman) 1775. 3 vols., 8°.

Lettre sur l'origine du titre de marquis en France; Tobiésen-Duby. (See: Journal des Savans, 1789. 4°.)

Carte de l'état actuel des duchés et comtés pairie; Brion. (See: La France analytique II.)

Essai sur les apanages; (Du Vaucel.) 2 vols., 4°.

Discours, mémoires et plaidoyés et autres actes touchant l'origine des ducs et pairs de France. 4 vols., fol.

Des pairs de France; (de Pensey) 1816. 8°.

Histoire des pairs de France; de Courcelles 1826. 12 vols., 4°.

De la pairie, de la noblesse, etc.; Berryer, 1831.

L'hérédité de la pairie; Berryer 1831.

Traité des apanages; Dupin 1835. 12°.

Curiosités nobiliaires et héraldiques; Chassant 1858. 8°.

La noblesse en France; de Barthélemy 1858. 18°.

Recherches sur la noblesse maternelle; de Barthélemy 1861. 8°.

Nouvelles observations sur la noblesse maternelle; de Barthélemy 1865. 8°.

Les ducs et les duchés français; de Barthélemy 1867. 8°.

La noblesse de France sous l'ancienne monarchie; Louandre 1880. 18°.

Histoire de la principauté de Donzère. (See: Bibliographie du Dauphiné.)

www.ingramcontent.com/pod-product-compliance
Lightning Source LLC
Chambersburg PA
CBHW021441090426
42739CB00009B/1584